D0065781

A gift for:

_____

From:

_____

The
Strength
~of~
Character

Charles R. Swindoll

The Strength of Character *7 Essential Traits of a Remarkable Life*

Copyright © 2007 by Charles R. Swindoll, Inc.

Published by J. Countryman, a division of Thomas Nelson, Inc, Nashville, Tennessee 37214.

Compiled and edited by Terri Gibbs

Designed by LeftCoast Design, Portland Oregon.

www.thomasnelson.com

ISBN 13: 978-1-4041-0394-5　　Printed and bound in Belgium

Contents

❧

❧

Preface

*I*magine some scholarly historian in the distant future, probing ancient archives and peering into dim and dusty records for clues about a life in the past. Your life.

As he lays all the puzzle pieces on the table—the faded photographs, the curled pages of a journal, the accounts of your driving record, your academic achievements, and credit reports—he begins to draw conclusions about who you were and what you were all about. What factors might that researcher consider as he pulls together his report?

If he is wise, he will remember that you are a product of your time. All of us are. That's an important point to keep in mind when you're considering anyone's life. We cannot and must not separate a person from his or her times. Our moment in history and our unique, individual circumstances become the anvil upon which our character is forged and formed. We will either rise to the challenge of our times and make a difference, or we will remain stuck on the sidelines.

It was no accident that you were born into this particular era, at this very juncture of history in our nation and our world. God is looking for a man or woman, who will yield to His purposes and seize the day for His glory. He calls us His "workmanship" (Ephesians 2:10). He is hammering, filing, chiseling, and shaping us! Peter's second letter goes so far as to list some of the things included in this shaping process: diligence, faith, moral excellence, knowledge, self-control, perseverance, godliness, kindness, and love (2 Peter 1:5–7). In a word . . . *character*.

Character qualities in His children—that's God's relentless quest and He won't quit until He completes His checklist. You may feel unqualified, uneducated, untrained, under-gifted, or even unworthy. Yet, those are excellent qualifications for God to do a mighty work.

He is still looking for the man or woman who will believe Him, despite weaknesses and doubts, and become a mighty tool in His hand . . . an instrument of His purpose, a person with the strength of character.

CHARLES R. SWINDOLL

God is more concerned about our character

than our comfort. His goal is not to pamper

us physically but to perfect us spiritually.

The Strength of
Courage

To walk by faith

requires courage.

❧

How easy it is to be "average."
The ranks of the mediocre are crowded
with status-quo thinkers and predictable
workers. How rare are those
who live differently!

Courage Beyond the Common

A Whack on the Side of the Head is a book on how to break the inertia and unlock your mind for innovative thinking. By adopting a creative outlook, as Roger von Oech, the author of the book, points out, we open ourselves to new possibilities and change. But that requires thinking outside the prison of common boundaries. It requires courage.

Johann Gutenberg is a superb example. What did he do? He simply combined two previously unconnected ideas to create an innovation. He refused to limit his thinking to the singular purpose of the wine press or to the solitary use of the coin punch. One day he entertained an idea no one else had ever thought of: "What if I took a bunch of coin punches and put them under the force of the wine press so that they left their images on paper instead of metal?" From that innovative thought the printing press was born.

THE QUEST FOR CHARACTER

Go for It!

❦

*H*ow difficult it is for some folks to imagine, to envision, to be enraptured by the unseen, all hazards and hardships notwithstanding. I'm almost convinced that one of the reasons mountain climbers connect themselves to one another with a rope is to keep the one on the end from going home. The guys out front never consider that an option . . . but those in the rear, well, let's just say they are the last to get a glimpse of the glory.

I've been thinking recently about how glad I am that certain visionaries refused to listen to the short-sighted doomsayers who could only see as far as the first obstacle. I'm glad, for example,

➤ that Luther refused to back down when the Church doubled her fists and clenched her teeth;

➤ that Michelangelo kept pounding and painting, regardless of those negative put-downs;

➤ that the distinguished Julliard School of Music would see beyond the leg braces and wheelchair and admit an unlikely violin student named Perlman;

➤ that our Lord Jesus held nothing back when He left heaven, lived on earth, and went for it—all the way to the cross—and beyond.

You could add to the list. You may even belong *on* the list. Is so, hats off to you!

THE QUEST FOR CHARACTER

Even if your day is shadowed by
fear or uncertainty, God is with you . . .
as close as your heartbeat,
as near as your next breath.

Step Out Into the Red Sea

❦

Want to know the shortest route to ineffectiveness? Start running scared. Try to cover every base at all times. Become paranoid. Think about every possible peril, focus on the dangers, concern yourself with the "what ifs" instead of the "why nots?" Take no chances. Say no to courage and yes to caution. Expect the worst. Let fear run wild. Keep yourself safely tucked away in the secure nest of inaction and before you know it the "paralysis of analysis" will set in. So will loneliness, and finally isolation. No thanks!

How much better to take on a few ornery bears and lions, like David did. They ready us for giants like Goliath. How much more thrilling to step out into the Red Sea like Moses and watch God part the waters. Sure makes for exciting stuff to talk about while trudging around a miserable wilderness for the next forty years.

Guard your heart from overprotection!

THE QUEST FOR CHARACTER

Empowered

❧

*J*esus reaches out to us and offers a helping hand
to lead us through life. Because He remains "the same
yesterday, today, and forever," no storm is too devastating,
no climb is too steep. He can handle it. He can get you
through. As a matter of fact He can empower you with
supernatural strength in the process.

There's an old translation of the New Testament
by Charles B. Williams, titled *The New Testament in the
Language of the People.* In that excellent translation a
footnote at Philippians 4:13 reads, "I have power for
all things through Him who puts a dynamo in me."

Isn't that great? When Christ comes into your life,
He places a dynamo there. It's a power pack that can be
adjusted and adapted, tightening up when necessary or
letting out slack. It can release or hold back, depending
on the terrain. It can control. It can keep things on a
fairly tranquil plane. How? Why? Because He is present.
That's the ticket—His presence hard at work deep
within your being.

GETTING THROUGH THE TOUGH STUFF

It Takes Courage

*D*eep within, we imagine ourselves as a mixture of Patrick Henry, Davy Crockett, John Wayne, and the prophet Daniel! But the truth of the matter is that most of us would do anything to keep from being different. We'd much rather blend into the woodwork. One of our greatest fears is being ostracized, rejected by "the group."

There are other fears—fear of being made to look foolish, fear of being talked about and misunderstood. Rather than rugged individualists, we are more like Gulliver of old, tied down and immobilized by tiny strands of fear, real or imagined. The result is both predictable and tragic: loss of courage.

It takes courage to think alone, to resist alone, to stand alone—especially when the crowd seems so safe, so right.

Let me suggest four thoughts to help bolster your courage:

1. *"I am responsible."* I said that to myself so many times in the Marine Corps that I got sick of hearing myself say it! Today I still repeat those three words.

2. *"I must not forget."* We must not forget the Lord our God and what He has done for us.

3. *"I am accountable."* I am accountable to God whether I am in Asia, at the tip of South America, or at the North Pole.

4. *"I get my standard and security from God."* Not from my friend, not from my business, not even from within myself. Christ is my surety.

Remember. Just because "everybody's doing it" doesn't mean it's either safe or right. You keep flying high above the crowd. Up there it doesn't just seem safe and right, it *is* safe and right.

LIVING ABOVE THE LEVEL OF MEDIOCRITY

Character is simply long habit continued.

PLUTARCH

Faith Leads to Action

❦

$\mathcal{L}$iving out your faith at the office or in that university dorm or in your high school may feel pretty lonely. Walking by faith and honoring the Lord in your factory or in your profession or in the military may seem futile at times. In fact, in your own lifetime, you may never know the significance of your walk of faith. But God will use you in His special plan for your life, just as He has countless others.

I've sat in the castle where Luther hid while he was translating the Scriptures into the German vernacular. I've looked out his window and thought about Luther as he sat in that very room, faithfully discharging his task, knowing that if the church leaders found him they would put him to death. Luther, Calvin, Savonarola, Knox, Wesley . . . on and on the list goes, right up to today. While the world mocked, God honored them. And that still happens today.

Just because something is God's will doesn't mean people will understand. On the contrary, most never do. But that's part of the mystery. Faith leads to action, requiring release and risk.

THE MYSTERY OF GOD'S WILL

Being Relates to Character

W hat we want to *do* is not nearly as important as what we want to *be*. Doing is usually concerned with a vocation or career, *how we make a living*.

Being is much deeper. It relates to character, who we are, and *how we make a life*. Doing is tied with accomplishments and tangible things—like salary and trophies. Being, on the other hand, has more to do with intangibles, much of which can't be measured by objective yardsticks and impressive awards.

DAVID: A MAN OF PASSION AND DESTINY

Man looks at the outward appearance,

but the LORD looks at the heart.

1 SAMUEL 16:7

The LORD has set apart the godly
man [and woman] for Himself.

PSALM 4:3

Set Apart for God

❧

*A*ll who choose godliness live in a crucible. The tests *will* come.

But all is not lost. Far from it! Our great hope and assurance is that the One in us is greater than the one in the world. We do not face such a formidable enemy that we cannot fight him or stand firm and secure in our decision. Our Lord is the God of hope.

When you determine that you are going to count for Christ as a godly man, a godly woman, a godly young person, when you determine to be a person sold out to God—not just a run-of-the-mill, mediocre Christian accepting Christ as a fire escape—you become the object of God's special attention. He says He "sets you apart" for Himself (Psalm 4:3). And the verse adds, "The Lord hears when I call to Him." Those two thoughts fit together. The godly often need to call upon God when the perils come. So He says, "I am here and I will answer. I will hear what you have to say."

MOSES: A MAN OF SELFLESS DEDICATION

Got Gumption?

❦

We don't hear much about *gumption* any more.
Too bad, since we need it more than ever these days.
Gumption means being disciplined one day at a time.
Rather than focusing on the whole enchilada, take it
in bite-size chunks. The whole of any objective can
overwhelm even the most courageous.

Writing a book? Do so one page at a time.

Running a marathon? Those 26-plus miles are run
one step at a time.

Trying to master a new language? Try one word at a
time.

There are 365 days in the average year. Divide any
project by 365 and none seem all that intimidating, do
they? It will take daily discipline, not annual discipline.

THE QUEST FOR CHARACTER

Today is unique! It has never occurred
before and it will never be repeated.

At midnight it will end,
quietly, suddenly, totally.

Forever.

But the hours between now and then
are opportunities with eternal possibilities.

All who live risk something.

To laugh is to risk appearing the fool.

To weep is to risk appearing sentimental.

To reach out for another is to risk involvement.

To expose feelings is to risk exposing your true self.

To love is to risk not being loved in return.

To hope is to risk despair.

To try is to risk failure.

Trust God Completely

❦

We Americans use a number of words to describe a predicament. If you're from the East, you probably know about "being in a pinch." If you like to cook, you're "in a jam," or "in a pickle." If you're from the South, you're "between a rock and a hard place." There are all manner of such expressions. . . . It may be that right now you find yourself in a predicament.

So what lessons can you learn when you find yourself in a predicament? It might well be that the *only* solution to your predicament is a miracle. What should your response be?

Most people are prone to say, "God helps the *helpless*!" As long as we're helping ourselves, who needs God? It's when we reach the end of our tether, and we're dangling out in space, that we finally cry out, "God, help me!" And God says, "I will. *Let go*." What's our normal response? "Is there anybody else up there who can help me?" Letting go works against human nature. But God wants us to do just that—to freefall into His everlasting arms and trust completely in Him. It's all a part of His plan.

MOSES: A MAN OF SELFLESS DEDICATION

The Strength of
Self-Control

We pursue the
spiritual disciplines
for an audience of One.

The Three-Second Pause

❦

*T*he exercise of this discipline called self-control prevents desire from becoming dictator. For the person without Christ, the desires dictate and he or she obeys. Those in Christ, living under the authority of His Spirit and ruled by Him, are able to defy this once-powerful dictator. As a result, we experience a transforming change that others notice.

As for the tongue, we exercise verbal restraint. Where our diet is concerned, we exercise restraint at the dinner table. (And I leave the ice cream in the freezer!) Pertaining to the temper, we exercise emotional restraint. As it relates to our thoughts, we exercise mental restraint. In terms of sexual lust, we exercise moral restraint. All of us have areas that tempt us more than others, so we must give ourselves over to the Spirit's authority. He steps in and empowers us to hold back before we take steps to satisfy our impulse or our desire.

Let's get practical. I have found that a three-second pause can make all the difference. Just as an impulse hits me, I decide to wait just three seconds before taking any action. During that pause, I do a quick assessment of what the consequences might be. Would this action be something that I would be embarrassed about later? Not all impulses are bad; some are good. Those three seconds have kept me out of a lot of hot water over the years.

SO YOU WANT TO BE LIKE CHRIST

I am frequently amazed by how effectively the Lord provides self-control when I need it. As I release the struggle to Him, He takes over. Every time.

*The purpose of self-control is that
we may be fit for God, fit for ourselves,
and fit to be servants of others.*

*It is not a rigid, religious practice—
discipline for discipline's sake.*

*It is not dull drudgery aimed at
exterminating laughter and joy.*

*It is the doorway to true joy, true
liberation from the stifling slavery
of self-interest and fear.*

MAXIE DUNHAM

This mastery of self is an incredibly difficult discipline, but it's the path to freedom.

Every Moment Matters

❧

Life on earth is really nothing more than a string
of moments, one after another. And I do not want my
testimony for Jesus Christ to be shattered by a single
moment of indulging my flesh. I don't want *one moment*
of rage or pride or arrogance to cast a shadow over a
lifetime of walking with my Lord. Frankly, I fear that
possibility. And do you know what? I want to fear that
possibility. When I stop fearing it, I am in grave danger.

Moses: A Man of Selfless Dedication

Let's Practice Restraint

Restraining ourselves—self-control—is so important that God lists it as a fruit of the Spirit.

Removing restraint from your life may seem like an exciting adventure, but it inevitably leads to tragedy. It's a lot like removing the brakes from your car. That may be daring and filled with thrills for a while, but injury is certain. Take away the brakes and your life, like your car, is transformed into an unguided missile—destined for disaster.

The fruit of the Spirit is . . . self-control.

GALATIANS 5:22–23

FIVE MEANINGFUL MINUTES A DAY

Controlling Those Cravings

*I*t is impossible to come to terms with moral purity without dealing with some practical facts related to the body—our flesh-and-blood appetites that crave satisfaction.

- ➤ We are to present our bodies as living sacrifices to God. (Romans 12:1)

- ➤ We are instructed *not* to yield any part of our bodies as instruments of unrighteousness to sin. (Romans 6:12–13)

- ➤ Our bodies are actually "members of Christ"; they belong to Him. (1 Corinthians 6:15)

You see, these bodies of ours can easily lead us off course. It isn't that the body itself is evil; it's just that it possesses any number of appetites that are ready to respond to the surrounding stimuli . . . all of which are terribly appealing and temporarily satisfying.

STRENGTHENING YOUR GRIP

The quest for character requires
that certain things be kept in the
heart as well as kept from the heart.

An unguarded heart spells disaster.
A well-guarded heart means survival.

❦

The Secret to Winning

*ike many Corinthian citizens, Paul was a sports fan.
He often inserted athletic terms in his writings. Here is
a case in point.

*Do you not know that those who run in a race all run, but
only one receives the prize? Run in such a way that you
may win. Everyone who competes in the games exercises
self-control in all things. They, then, do it to receive a
perishable wreath, but we an imperishable. Therefore I
run in such a way, as not without aim; I box in such a
way, as not beating the air; but I discipline my body and
make it my slave, so that, after I have preached to others,
I myself will not be disqualified.*

1 CORINTHIANS 9:24–27

The Isthmian Games, held every two years near
Corinth, were almost as popular as the Olympic Games.
Competitions included running, wrestling, and boxing,
from which Paul drew this particular set of word pictures.
Using images familiar to every Corinthian would help
him establish the link between discipline and excellence.

Paul's hope is that we will run with purpose. Not that we will merely run the race of life, but, that we will run to win. He desires for all of us to become winners, not merely runners.

So, what's the secret? How do winners compete? "Everyone who competes in the games exercises self-control in all things." It's always required the same secret: discipline. Those who run to win exercise restraint over their impulses and emotions and desires. Olympic hopefuls are this very day watching their diet, getting sufficient sleep, and training their bodies in just the right way for just the right amount of time. They are not fudging on anything that might hedge their performance on the track, on the bike, in the pool, or in the ring. And they measure the consequences of every impulse to judge whether it will assist them or hinder them from fulfilling the purpose of competition: winning the gold.

So You Want to Be Like Christ

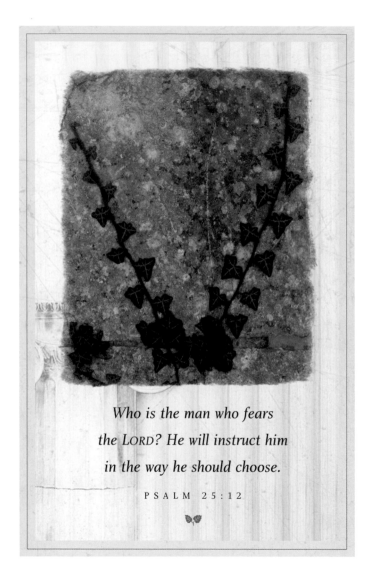

*Who is the man who fears
the LORD? He will instruct him
in the way he should choose.*

PSALM 25:12

Free to Choose

❧

$\mathcal{B}$y making us in His image, God gave us capacities not given to other forms of life. Ideally, He made us to know Him, to love Him, and to obey Him. He did not put rings in our noses to pull us around like oxen, nor did He create us with strings permanently attached to our hands and feet like human marionettes.

No, He gave us freedom to make choices.

FIVE MEANINGFUL MINUTES A DAY

Walking in Purity

🦋

$\mathcal{T}$hink back to 1939. That was the year *Gone with the Wind* was released, including in its script a scandal-making, four-letter word that raised the eyebrows of moviegoers around the world. Has there been much change since '39? Do four-letter words still create scandals? What a joke!

Pornography shops are now in every major American city. Hard-core X-rated films are now available on cable television as well as in most hotels. We have reached an all-time low with "kiddie porn" and "love" murders (yes, the actual crime) now captured on film. Even prime-time TV isn't exempt from intimate bedroom scenes, verbal explosions of profanity, and a rather frequent diet of so-called humor regarding sexual intercourse, homosexuality, nudity, and various parts of the human anatomy.

And all of this assaults the senses with such relentless regularity that we need the power of God to walk in purity.

God wants you to be holy and pure, and to keep
clear of all sexual sin so that each of you will marry
in holiness and honor—not in lustful passion as the
heathen do, in their ignorance of God and his ways.

1 THESSALONIANS 4:1–5 TLB

The Roman world of Paul's day was a cultural climate much like ours today. Impurity was viewed either with passive indifference or open favor. Christians back then (and now) were like tiny islands of morality surrounded by vast oceans of illicit sex and promiscuity. Knowing the current of temptation that swirled around them, he counseled them to "abstain"—an open and shut case for total abstention from sexual immorality. The same is as true today as it was in the first century. "Christian holiness," says Paul, "requires total abstinence from *porneias* ("sexual immorality," "fornication").

In our day of moral decline, it is easy to begin thinking that purity is some unachievable, outdated standard from the misty past of yesteryear. *Not so!*

STRENGTHENING YOUR GRIP

God has not called us for the purpose

of impurity, but in sanctification.

The Purpose of Discipline

❦

"I discipline my body and make it my slave."

1 CORINTHIANS 9:27

$\mathcal{T}$he purpose of this discipline over the body is, as the literal Greek would put it, "to enslave it." Like an athlete, we have to show our bodies who's boss. That includes saying no to its whining wish that we indulge its every whim. The point of disciplined self-control is to make the body serve us rather than the other way around.

FIVE MEANINGFUL MINUTES A DAY

The Benefit of Boundaries

Our society has gorged itself on the sweet taste of success. We've filled our plates from a buffet of books that range from dressing for success to investing for success. We've passed the newsstands and piled our plates higher with everything from *Gentleman's Quarterly* and *Vogue*, to the *Wall Street Journal* and *Time*. When we've devoured these, we have turned our ravenous appetites toward expensive, success-oriented seminars. We've gobbled down stacks of notebooks, CD albums, and video tapes in our hunger for greater success.

The irony of all this is that instead of fulfillment, we experience the bloated sensation of being full of ourselves—*our* dreams, *our* goals, *our* plans, *our* projects, *our* accomplishments. The result of this all-you-can-eat appetite is not contentment. It's nausea. How terribly dissatisfying!

Interestingly, very few address that which most folks want but seldom find in their pursuit of success, and that is contentment, fulfillment, satisfaction. Rarely, if ever, are we offered boundaries and encouraged to say, "Enough is enough."

HOPE AGAIN

Rest and Restoration

❦

We can learn a lesson from nature. A period of rest always follows a harvest; the land must be allowed time to renew itself. Constant production without restoration depletes resources and, in fact, diminishes the quality of what is produced.

Super-achievers and workaholics, take heed! If the light on your inner dashboard is flashing red, you are carrying too much too far too fast. If you don't pull over, you'll be sorry . . . and so will all those who love you. If you are courageous enough to get out of that fast lane and make some needed changes, you will show yourself wise.

THE QUEST FOR CHARACTER

Sow a thought, reap an act.

Sow an act, reap a habit.

Sow a habit, reap character.

Sow character, reap a destiny.

A Brief Appraisal

❧

Well . . . how's it going in your life? Let's take a brief appraisal. Pause long enough to review and reflect. Try to be honest as you answer these questions. I'll warn you; they may hurt a little.

➤ Am I enjoying most of my activities or just enduring them?

➤ Have I deliberately taken time on several occasions this year for personal restoration?

➤ Are my meals choked down or do I take sufficient time to taste and enjoy my food?

➤ Do I give myself permission to relax, to have leisure, to be quiet?

➤ Would other people think I am working too many hours and/or living under too much stress?

➤ Am I occasionally boring and often preoccupied?

➤ Am I staying physically fit? Do I consider my body important enough to maintain a nourishing diet, to give it regular exercise, to get enough sleep, to shed those excess pounds?

➤ How is my sense of humor?

➤ Is God being glorified by the schedule I keep . . . or is He getting the leftovers of my energy?

THE QUEST FOR CHARACTER

The mouth of the righteous utters wisdom,

and his tongue speaks justice.

PSALM 37:30

Let's Watch What We Say

❧

How much hurt, how much damage can be done by chance remarks! Our unguarded tongues can deposit germ-thoughts of hurt, humiliation, and hate into tender minds that fester, become full-blown infections, and ultimately spread disease throughout another life. With little regard for the other person's vulnerability, we have the power to initiate a violent emotional earthquake by merely making a few statements that rip and tear like shrapnel in the person's head. Such destructive words are like sending 800 volts through 110 wire.

I find help and guidance in Solomon's proverbs. He mentions "tongue," "lips," "mouth," and "words" a little less than 150 times—that's just under five times a chapter. Over and over he exhorts us to watch what we say, when we say it, and how we say it. Offense or healing can come from the same mouth—from the same heart. Proverbs has thirty-one chapters. How about reading a chapter a day for the next month and practicing a little verbal self-control?

THE QUEST FOR CHARACTER

Stop Striving for More!

❧

Contentment is something we must learn. It isn't a trait we're born with. But the question is *how?*

First, it really helps us to quit striving for more if we read the eternal dimension into today's situation. We entered life empty-handed; we leave it the same way. I never saw a hearse pulling a U-Haul trailer!

Second, it also helps us model contentment if we'll boil life down to its essentials and try to simplify our lifestyle. First Timothy 6:8 spells out those essentials. "And if we have food and covering, with these we shall be content"—something to eat, something to wear, and a roof over our heads. Everything beyond that we'd do well to consider as extra.

You see, society's plan of attack is to create dissatisfaction, to convince us that we must be in a constant pursuit for something "out there" that is sure to bring us happiness. When you reduce that lie to its lowest level, it is saying that contentment is impossible without striving for more. God's Word offers the exact opposite advice: Contentment is possible when we *stop* striving for more.

My bottom-line interest is helping you see the true values in life and to see through the mask of our world system and the power of advertising. I recall hearing some pretty good counsel on how to overrule those television commercials that attempt to convince us we need this product or that new appliance to be happy. The guy suggested that every time we begin to feel that persuasive tug, we ought to shout back at the tube at the top of our voices: "Who are you kidding?"

It really works. My whole family and I tried it one afternoon during a televised football game. Not once did I feel dissatisfied with my present lot or sense the urge to jump up and go buy something. Our dog almost had a canine coronary; but other than that, the results were great.

STRENGTHENING YOUR GRIP

Eternal Rewards

In his letter to the Corinthians, the apostle Paul mentions "a perishable wreath."

Everyone who competes in the games exercises self-control in all things. They then do it to receive a perishable wreath, but we an imperishable.

1 CORINTHIANS 9:25

The Isthmian Games were centuries old, starting with the Greeks and carried on by the Romans. By the first century the prize was a crown made of woven pine fronds in honor of Poseidon, god of the sea. But that's not all. Victors were treated like royalty both at the games and in their hometowns. Officials would break a large opening in the city wall and fill it with a brass covering bearing the engraved name of the winner. His debts were canceled, and he was allowed to live tax-free for the rest of his life. Sometimes he would be given a lifetime supply of food, so that he could literally rest on his laurels.

But stop and think: as impressive and enjoyable as those rewards were, they were all temporary, all perishable —the brass will tarnish, the wreath will wither, the fame will fade. And at the end of life, temporal comforts will mean nothing. Paul pointed out that, as valuable as the leafy crown was for the moment, it cannot compare to the eternal rewards for which we strive. We run a race called life for a prize of unimaginable worth, and to win it we must exercise the discipline of restraint— self-control.

So You Want to Be Like Christ

The Strength of
Honesty

*Christ not only lived an
exemplary life, He also makes
it possible for us to do the same.*

With authority comes the need for accountability. With prosperity comes the need for integrity.

The Best Way to Be Honest

*D*id you know that ever since 1811 (when someone who had defrauded the government anonymously sent $5 to Washington D. C.) the U. S. Treasury has operated a *Conscience Fund*? Since that time almost $3.5 million has been received from guilt-ridden citizens.

The answer to dishonesty is a return to honesty. *Integrity* may be an even better word. It boils down to an internal decision to guard the heart against greed.

One of the reasons Christianity is so appealing is the hope it provides. Christ doesn't offer a technique on rebuilding *your* life. He offers you *His* life—His honesty, His integrity. Not a lot of rules and don't's and threats. But sufficient power to counteract our dishonest bent. He calls it "a new nature, pure and undefiled" (1 Peter 1:4)—thoroughly honest. Some would tell you that believing in Jesus Christ—trusting Him to break old habits and make you honest—means committing intellectual suicide. No way! It is not only the best way to be honest, it's the *only* way.

THE QUEST FOR CHARACTER

Don't Lie to Yourself

*E*ver so slightly, invisible moral and ethical germs can invade, bringing the beginning stages of a terminal disease. No one can tell by looking, for it happens imperceptibly. It's slower than a clock and far more silent. There are no chimes, not even a persistent ticking. An oversight here, a compromise there, a deliberate looking the other way, a softening, a yawn, a nod, a nap, a habit . . . a destiny. And before we know it, a chunk of character falls into the sea. What was once "no big deal" becomes, in fact, bigger than life itself.

Take time today to scrutinize your life. Think hard. Don't lie to yourself. Ask and answer a few tough questions. Compare "the way we were" with "the way we are." Look within the walls of your moral standard, your commitment to ethical excellence. Any termites in the timber? Any erosions taking place that you haven't bothered to notice? Just because the changes are silent and slow doesn't mean things aren't deteriorating.

THE QUEST FOR CHARACTER

Want a challenge? Start modeling the truth . . .
the whole truth and nothing but the
truth, so help you God.

Think truth.

Confess truth.

Face truth.

Love truth.

Pursue truth.

Walk truth.

Talk truth.

Ah, that last one! That's a good place to begin.
From this day forward, deliberately, consciously,
and conscientiously speak the truth. Start
practicing gut-level authenticity.

❦

Let's Be Authentic

Webster's dictionary defines the term *authentic* by suggesting three things "authentic" is not: It is *not* imaginary, it is *not* false, it is *not* an imitation. Today we would say that being authentic means not being phony.

Let's work hard at being real. This means we are free to question, to admit failure or weakness, to confess wrong, to declare the truth. When a person is authentic, he or she does not have to win or always be in the top ten or make a big impression or look super-duper pious. . . .

Authentic people usually enjoy life more than most. They don't take themselves so seriously. They actually laugh and cry and think more freely because they have nothing to prove—no big image to protect, no role to play. They have no fear of being found out, because they're not hiding anything. Let's make this a priority!

STRENGTHENING YOUR GRIP

A Prayer for Authenticity

Oh, God, above all things, help us to be authentic people, not actors on a stage, filled with ourselves and eager for applause.

Help us to be genuine to the core of our faith.

Help us to admit hypocrisy in ourselves.

Strengthen us to expose that which is counterfeit.

Give us the courage to be honest with ourselves and to shoot straight with each other.

GETTING THROUGH THE TOUGH STUFF

How important is the heart!

It is there that character is formed.

It alone holds the secrets of true success.

Guard Your Heart

❧

$\mathcal{A}$s I wade through the success propaganda written today, again and again the focus of attention is on one's outer self—how smart I can appear, what a good impression I can make, how much I can own or how totally I can control or how fast I can be promoted or . . . or . . . or. Nothing I read—and I mean *nothing*—places emphasis on the heart, the inner being, the seed plot of our thoughts, motives, decisions. Nothing, that is, except Scripture.

Interestingly, the Bible says little about success, but a lot about heart, the place where true success originates. No wonder Solomon challenges his readers:

> *Above all else, guard your heart,*
> *for it is the wellspring of life.*
>
> PROVERBS 4:23, NIV

That's right—*guard* it. Put a sentinel on duty. Watch it carefully. Protect it. Keep it clean.

THE QUEST FOR CHARACTER

If you don't take God seriously,
there's no need to take seriously such
character traits as submission, faithfulness,
purity, humility, repentance, and honesty.

God Knows Us and Loves Us

*F*rom a distance we're all beautiful people. Well-dressed.
Nice smile, friendly looking, cultured, under control,
at peace. But what a different picture when someone
comes up close and gets in touch! What appeared so
placid is really a mixture: winding roads of insecurity
and uncertainty, maddening gusts of lust, greed, self-
indulgence, pathways of pride glazed over with a slick
layer of hypocrisy; all of this shrouded in a cloud of fear
of being found out. From a distance we dazzle . . . up close
we're tarnished. Put enough of us together and we may
resemble an impressive mountain range. But when you get
down into the shadowy crevices . . . the Alps we ain't.

I'm convinced that's why our Lord means so much to
us. He scrutinizes our path. He is intimately acquainted
with all our ways. All things are open and laid bare
before Him: our darkest secret, our deepest shame, our
stormy past, our worst thought, our hidden motive, our
vilest imagination . . . even our vain attempts to cover the
ugly with snow-white beauty. He comes up close. He sees
it all. Best of all, He loves us still.

THE QUEST FOR CHARACTER

Living in truth is making the right choices.

The secret, of course, is making

the right choices every day.

Don't Be Phony!

❦

*T*he apostle Paul wrote to the believers in Rome with great fervor as he exhorted them to "let love be without hypocrisy" (Romans 12:9). He urged for action to match words.

Here's the point. . . . Don't be phony. Say what you mean, and mean what you say. And when you're with one group, say the same thing you said when you were with a previous group. All the while, be sure your life squares with what you say you believe. When it doesn't, admit it. Just come out and say so!

Mark Twain was reportedly once asked, "What's the difference between a liar and a person who tells the truth?" Wisely, Twain replied, "Very simple. A liar has to have a better memory."

GETTING THROUGH THE TOUGH STUFF

The Drudgery of Duplicity

❧

*T*heater was one of the hallmarks of Greek culture in
Jesus' day. The practice was for one actor to play multiple
roles on stage. He disguised himself with a series of masks,
which he would interchange off stage to the delight of the
audience. He would come from the side of the stage with
a smiling mask in front of his face as he spoke his comedy
lines. The crowd would laugh uproariously over his
humorous monologue, watching as the actor raced off the
scene to don a frowning mask of tragic expression. With that,
the actor would return and speak lines of solemn thought
and sadness and, in a sense, answer back to the audience.
Not surprisingly, the actor was called a "hypocrite."

Over time the word took on more negative connotations,
and eventually it evolved into the word Jesus used to pinpoint
the "double-masked" pretense that marked the Pharisees.

That type of pretending to be what one is not is
consistently and forcefully condemned in Scripture.
Every time our God takes the time to address false piety
or duplicity of character, He roundly condemns it.

GETTING THROUGH THE TOUGH STUFF

An Open Honesty

❦

Remember Doubting Thomas? Of course you do. Talk about a bad rap that stuck! My heart goes out to the poor guy. I'd rather think of him, thanks to one astute Bible scholar's analysis, as Reflective Thomas.

He's the one honest disciple who didn't check his brain at the synagogue door. He had faith in his doubts when his questions weren't answered. He had the guts to question the crowd, to raise his hand and press for answers that made better sense. I call that kind of honesty not only reassuring but valiant. I would love to see the ranks of Christianity filled with more courageous believers willing to declare openly the struggles they have, to weep when they're hurting, to admit their doubts rather than deny them.

GETTING THROUGH THE TOUGH STUFF

An Honest Admission

*H*ow unsearchable are God's judgments. How unfathomable are His ways (Romans 11:33). That doesn't mean He's not in touch, out of control, and doesn't have a plan. It just means He isn't obligated to explain Himself. And because He doesn't reveal everything, we're left with three very honest words, which are helpful coming from the lips of otherwise proud people.

And what are those three words? *I don't know.*

In the final analysis, God knows, and He does all things well. He is in charge. I am the clay; He is the Potter. I am the disciple; He is the Lord. I am the sheep; He is the Shepherd. I am the servant; He is the Master. That means I am to submit myself. I am to humble myself under His mighty hand. I must be willing to adjust my life to His choices for me, to listen, to learn, to adapt to His leading wherever it may go whether I'm comfortable, happy, or healthy.

JOB: A MAN OF HEROIC ENDURANCE

Character Qualities Endure

*T*imes do change things . . . sometimes drastically.
Styles change, as do expectations, salaries, communication
systems, even relating to people.

But some things have no business changing. Like
respect for authority, personal integrity, wholesome
thoughts, pure words, holy living, distinct roles of
masculinity and femininity, commitment to Christ,
love for family, and authentic servanthood. Character
qualities are never up for grabs.

Times must change. But character? Not on your life!

THE QUEST FOR CHARACTER

Walking with God doesn't guarantee
we'll live longer, but it does
help us live better.

And deeper.

And broader.

The Strength of
Determination

*J esus promised us an abundant
life. Abundant with challenges,
running over with possibilities.*

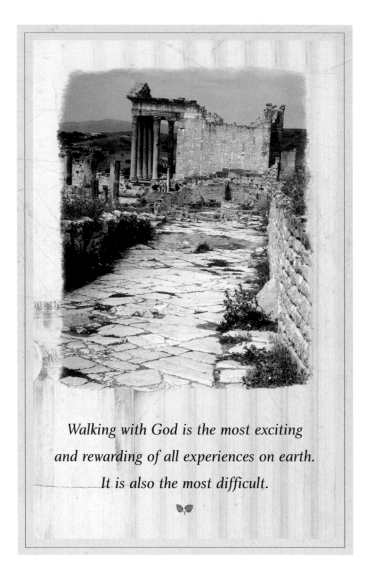

Walking with God is the most exciting
and rewarding of all experiences on earth.
It is also the most difficult.

Determination and Diligence

I find more encouragement from God's Word than any other source of information when it comes to the importance of personal dedication and determination.

The Lord assures me that His *glory* is my goal (1 Corinthians 10:31), not man's approval.

When He tells me to love, He tells me to do it *fervently* (1 Peter 4:8).

When maintaining a friendship, it is to be *devotedly* (Romans 12:10).

When seeing a person in need, we are to bear his or her burden *sacrificially* (Galatians 6:1–2), not at a safe distance.

When it comes to work, we are to be *disciplined* (2 Thessalonians 3:7–8) and *diligent* (1 Thessalonians 2:9).

The Scriptures are replete with exhortations to go above and beyond the required call of duty—to a dedication of life that thrives on excellence. Don't be afraid of determination and diligence. Such dedication is not only rare, it's downright contagious!

THE QUEST FOR CHARACTER

The traits we remember and admire
most about David were shaped while he
lived like a fugitive in the wilderness. Great
character, like massive roots, grows deep when
water is sparse and winds are strong. The
psalms we turn to the most often emerged
from a broken heart while tears wouldn't
stop and questions remained unanswered.

❧

Enduring Like Christ

❧

$\mathcal{T}$he most misunderstood individual who ever lived was Jesus Christ. Critics joked about the circumstances of His birth.

They disputed His divine origin with ethnic jeering and vicious taunts, even to the point of accusing Him of belonging to Satan.

They scorned His purposes.

They reviled His teachings.

They were suspicious of His motives, critical of His methods, and angered by His message.

Ultimately, the Jewish leaders conspired with the Roman officials to put Him to death. That explains what the apostle John meant when he wrote, "The Light shines in the darkness, and the darkness did not comprehend it. . . . He came to His own, and those who were His own did not receive Him" (John 1:5, 11). Christ came into an uncomprehending darkness where He met nothing but unbending misunderstanding.

Yet, in spite of being misunderstood, He endured. You can too.

GETTING THROUGH THE TOUGH STUFF

Strength of Character ❧

Creativity and Tenacity

❦

On May 24, 1965, a thirteen-and-a-half-foot boat slipped quietly out of the marina at Falmouth, Massachusetts. Its destination? England. It would be the smallest craft ever to make the voyage. Its name? *Tinkerbelle.* Its pilot? Robert Manry, a copyeditor for the *Cleveland Plain Dealer,* who felt that ten years at the desk was enough boredom for a while. So he took a leave of absence to fulfill his secret dream.

Manry was afraid . . . not of the ocean, but of all those people who would try to talk him out of the trip. So he didn't share it with many, just some relatives and especially his wife Virginia, his greatest source of support.

The trip? Anything but pleasant. He spent harrowing nights of sleeplessness trying to cross shipping lanes without getting run over and sunk. Weeks at sea caused his food to become tasteless. Loneliness led to terrifying hallucinations. His rudder broke three times. Storms swept him overboard, and had it not been for the rope he had knotted around his waist, he would never have been able to pull himself back on board. Finally, after seventy-eight days alone at sea, he sailed into Falmouth, England.

During those nights at the tiller, he had fantasized about what he would do once he arrived. He expected simply to check into a hotel, eat dinner alone, then the next morning see if, perhaps, the Associated Press might be interested in his story. Was he in for a surprise! Word of his approach had spread far and wide. To his amazement, three hundred vessels, with horns blasting, escorted *Tinkerbelle* into port. And forty thousand people stood screaming and cheering him to shore.

Robert Manry, the copyeditor turned dreamer, became an overnight hero. His story has been told around the world. We need more Roberts who have the creativity and the tenacity to break with boredom and try the unusual.

THE QUEST FOR CHARACTER

Staying at the Task

Dreams are important, no question; yet they must be mixed with the patient discipline of staying at the tough tasks, regardless.

This is not the popular message we hear today. I was struck by this realization recently while browsing through a new bookstore not far from my home. As I wandered through the section on management and motivation, the titles made a bold statement about how society feels regarding patience and long-term diligence:

Passport to Prosperity

Winning Moves

True Greed

Winning Through Intimidation

The Art of Selfishness

Techniques that Take You to the Top

How to Get What You Really Want

Secrets to Quick Success

Who's kidding whom? In spite of all those eye-catching, cleverly worded titles, the so-called secret to quick *anything* beneficial is light-years removed from the truth. In the final analysis, the race is won by right objectives relentlessly pursued. Whether it is an athlete reaching the Super Bowl, parents rearing a houseful of kids, a young woman earning her Ph.D., or a gifted musician perfecting his skill on an instrument, hanging tough over the long haul is still the investment that pays the richest dividends. And, I might add, it brings the greatest joy.

LAUGH AGAIN

Without dreams, life becomes dull,
tedious, full of caution, inhibited.

People who know who they are, who
possess a clear sense of their mission, and
who understand God's plan and purpose for
their lives, are people who experience genuine
fulfillment. That doesn't mean they don't face
extreme obstacles. Rather, it means they have
learned to face those challenges in ways that
transform obstacles into opportunities.
Rather than stumbling over them,
they press on through them.

The way of the LORD is a
stronghold to the upright. . . .
The righteous will never be shaken.

PROVERBS 10:29–30

Responding in Obedience

When He has tried me, I shall come forth as gold.

The overarching will of God is not about geography.
(Where should I go?)

It is not about occupation. (Where should I work?)

It is not about exactly what car I should drive.
(What color do you prefer?)

The overarching, big-picture will of God is not
centered in the petty details of everyday life that we
worry over. The will of God is primarily and ultimately
concerned about our becoming like Christ. And in that
sense, the will of God is a test. When He's tried us, and
we have responded in obedience (even though we didn't
understand why), we will come forth as gold.

THE MYSTERY OF GOD'S WILL

Faith and Careful Planning

I'd like us to reflect on the tension between careful planning and full-hearted faith. Are they mutually exclusive? Not on your life! Yet to talk to some believers, you might be led to think otherwise.

I've counseled with unemployed men and women who tell me, "I'm just waiting on the Lord to provide a job."

"Fine," I reply. "And where have you placed your resumé?"

"Well, I'm not going that route. I'm just waiting on God."

"Oh really?" I say. "Then I hope you don't mind going hungry for awhile."

The old motto of soldiers during the Revolutionary War applies to many areas of life: "Trust in God, but keep your powder dry!" In other words, place your life in the Savior's hands, but stay at the ready. Do all that you can to prepare yourself for battle, understanding that the ultimate outcome rests with the Lord God.

To walk by faith does not mean you stop thinking. To trust God does not imply becoming slovenly or lazy or apathetic. What a distortion of biblical faith! You and

I need to trust God for our finances, but that is no
license to spend foolishly. You and I ought to trust God
for safety in the car, but we're not wise to pass on a blind
curve. We trust God for our health, but that doesn't mean
we can chain smoke, stay up half the night, and subsist
on potato chips and Twinkies without consequences.

Acting foolishly or thoughtlessly, expecting God
to bail you out if things go amiss, isn't faith at all. It is
presumption. Wisdom says, do all you can within your
strength, then trust Him to do what you cannot do, to
accomplish what you cannot accomplish. Faith and
careful planning go hand-in-hand. They always have.

MOSES: A MAN OF SELFLESS DEDICATION

*In our overpopulated world, it is easy
to underestimate the significance of one.
It is easy to underestimate the value of
you: your vote, your convictions, your
determination to say, "I stand against this."*

Does it matter if we get involved
or not? *It matters greatly—
it matters to your character!*

Going in God's Direction

*G*od's voice isn't all that difficult to hear. In fact, you almost have to be closing your eyes and stopping your ears to miss it. He sometimes shouts through our pain, whispers to us while we're relaxing on vacation, occasionally He sings to us in a song, and warns us through the sixty-six books of His written Word. It's right there, ink on paper. Count on it—that book will never lead you astray.

In addition to His unfailing source of wisdom, He has given you wise counselors, friends, acquaintances, parents, teachers, and mentors who have earned your love and respect through long years. Filter what you believe to be the will of God through their thoughts, their perspectives. Does your conviction about the direction you're headed grow, or are you seeing lots of red flags and caution signs? Before you undertake a major life-direction change, be very careful that it is God's voice, that it is God's call you are hearing.

MOSES: A MAN OF SELFLESS DEDICATION

God's Wilderness School

❧

We live today in a microwave culture. If it takes longer than five minutes to fix lunch, that's too long! In earlier days, you even had to wait for a TV set to warm up. Can you imagine? And you couldn't push a single button on your phone to call home on a pre-set number, you had to *dial* it . . . with your finger, for pity's sake. Talk about the stone age! I remember driving by a vacant lot some time ago, then going by the same corner several weeks later. Where there had been nothing but grass and weeds, empty beer cans, and trash just days before, there was now a huge warehouse, assembled from pre-fabricated sections, ready to receive goods.

That's the way life is today. Fast. Compressed. Condensed. Slam-bang-it's-done. Not so in God's wilderness schooling. When it comes to walking with God, there is no such thing as instant maturity. God doesn't mass produce His saints. He hand-tools each one, and it always takes longer than we expected. And it often hurts.

MOSES: A MAN OF SELFLESS DEDICATION

God knows what He is about, and
He pursues it with relentless determination.

Running with Resilience

※

*T*here is a long, demanding course to be run in life, most of which takes place in the trenches and without applause. I suggest we intensify our determination and head for the goal. Endurance is the secret.

How do we learn endurance? We learn it one day at a time. We learn it through consistent faith. If you want to replace excuses with fresh determination and procrastination with tough-minded perseverance, you need discipline. You need resiliency. You need faith.

God knows what He's about. If He has you sidelined, out of the action for awhile, He knows what He's doing. You just stay faithful . . . stay flexible . . . stay available. At the precise moment He will reach for you and launch you to His place of appointment.

There is a God-arranged plan for your life and regardless of your circumstances God is working out that plan. You can be sure it will be fabulous!

FIVE MEANINGFUL MINUTES A DAY

God's faithfulness is unconditional,
unending, and unswerving.

❦

The Strength of
Unselfishness

*S omeone who is truly
unselfish is generous with his
or her time and possessions,
energy and money.*

A joyful heart expresses itself
in greathearted generosity.

Giving with Gusto!

❧

A happy spirit takes the grind out of giving. A positive attitude makes sacrifice a pleasure. When the morale is high the motivation is strong. When there is joy down inside, no challenge seems too great.

And have you noticed how contagious such a spirit becomes? Not only do we feel the wind at our backs, others do as well. And when we are surrounded by that dynamic, a fresh surge of determination sweeps over us. You cannot stop it!

Can you recall the statement Paul makes in the second letter to the Corinthians? "God loves a cheerful giver" (2 Corinthians 9:7). The term *cheerful*, remember, comes from a Greek word, *hilaros*, from which we get our word *hilarious*. And it's placed first in the original statement. Literally, "for the *hilarious* giver God prizes." Why? Because hilarious givers give with gusto!

THE QUEST FOR CHARACTER

Give the Gift of Encouragement

*I*t snowed all day Thanksgiving. The ski slopes where we were staying in Colorado were absolutely beautiful and in perfect condition. I struck out on my first attempts at skiing with a positive mental attitude, thinking, "I'm going to be the first person who learned to ski without falling down. *The Guinness Book of World Records* will hear of this and write me up!"

Don't bother to check, I'm not in the book.

It was unbelievable! You've heard of the elephant man? On skis, I'm the rhinoceros man. It is doubtful that anyone else on planet earth has ever come down any ski slope more ways than I did. Or landed in more positions. Or did more creative things in the air before landing.

Working with me that humiliating day was the world's most encouraging ski instructor (yes, I had an instructor!) who set the new record in patience.

Never once did she lose her cool.

Never once did she laugh at me.

Never once did she call me "dummy."

Never once did she say, "You are absolutely impossible. I quit!"

That dear, gracious lady helped me up more times than I can number. She repeated the same basics time and again—like she had never said them before. Even though I was colder than an explorer in the Antarctic, irritable, impatient, and under the snow more than I was on it, she kept offering words of reassurance. That day God gave me a living, never-to-be-forgotten illustration of the value of encouragement. Had it not been for her spirit and her words, believe me, I would have hung 'em up and been back in the condo, warming my feet by the fire in less than an hour.

What is true for a novice on the snow once a year is all the more true for the people we meet every day. Harassed by demands and deadlines; bruised by worry, adversity, and failure; broken by disillusionment; and defeated by sin, they live somewhere between dull discouragement and sheer panic. All of us need encouragement, and the beautiful part about encouragement is this: *Anybody* can do it!

Strengthening Your Grip

Encouragement in Action

*H*ere are a few ideas to help spark an interest in putting encouragement into action.

➤ Observe and mention admirable character qualities you see in others, such as:

Punctuality	Thoroughness
Tactfulness	Diligence
Faithfulness	Honesty
Good Attitude	Compassion
Loyalty	Good Sense of Humor
Tolerance	Vision and Faith

➤ Correspondence, thank-you notes, small gifts with a note attached. Preferably not so much at birthdays or Christmas, but at unexpected times.

➤ Phone calls. Be brief and to the point. Express appreciation for something specific that you genuinely appreciate.

➤ Notice a job well done and say so.

➤ Cultivate a positive, reassuring attitude. Encouragement cannot thrive in a negative, squint-eyed atmosphere.

➤ Pick up the tab in a restaurant . . . provide free tickets to some event you know the person (or family) would enjoy . . . send flowers . . . give a gift of money when it seems appropriate.

➤ Be supportive to someone you know is hurting. Reach out without fear of what others may think or say.

A well-timed expression of encouragement is never forgotten. Never!

STRENGTHENING YOUR GRIP

*Reflect on God's numerous gifts
to you. It will increase your joy.*

Becoming a Generous Person

❧

*W*ant to become a generous person? Let me remind you of four simple suggestions that work for me:

1. *Reflect on God's gifts to you.* Hasn't He been good? Better than we deserve.

2. *Remind yourself of God's promises regarding generosity.* Call to mind a few biblical principles that promise the benefits of sowing bountifully.

3. *Examine your heart and your attitude.* Nobody but you can ask the hard questions, like:
   Is my giving proportionate to my income?
   Am I motivated by guilt or by contagious joy?
   If someone else knew the level of my giving to God's work, would I be a model to follow?
   Have I prayed about giving?

4. *Trust God to honor consistent generosity.* Here's the big step, but it's essential. When you really believe God is leading you to make a significant contribution—release your restraint and develop the habit of generosity.

THE QUEST FOR CHARACTER

You Have to Give It All Away

$\mathcal{L}$egend has it that a man was lost in the desert, just dying for a drink of water. He stumbled upon an old shack and as he glanced around he saw a pump about fifteen feet away—an old, rusty water pump. He stumbled over to it, grabbed the handle, and began to pump up and down, up and down. Nothing came out.

Disappointed, he staggered back. He noticed off to the side an old jug. He looked at it, wiped away the dirt and dust, and read a message that said, "You have to prime the pump with all the water in this jug, my friend. P. S.: Be sure you fill the jug again before you leave."

He popped the cork out of the jug and sure enough, there was water. It was almost full of water! Suddenly, he was faced with a decision. If he drank the water, he could live. Ah, but if he poured all the water in the old rusty pump, maybe it would yield fresh, cool water from down deep in the well, all the water he wanted.

He studied the possibility of both options. What should he do, pour it into the old pump and take a chance on fresh, cool water or drink what was in the old jug and ignore its message?

Reluctantly he poured all the water into the pump. The he grabbed the handle and began to pump . . . squeak, squeak, squeak. Still nothing came out! Squeak, squeak, squeak. A little bit began to dribble out, then a small stream, and finally it gushed! To his relief fresh, cool water poured out of the rusty pump. Eagerly, he filled the jug and drank from it. He filled it another time and once again drank its refreshing contents.

Then he filled the jug for the next traveler. He filled it to the top, popped the cork back on, and added this little note: "Believe me, it really works. You have to give it all away before you can get *anything* back."

LIVING ABOVE THE LEVEL OF MEDIOCRITY

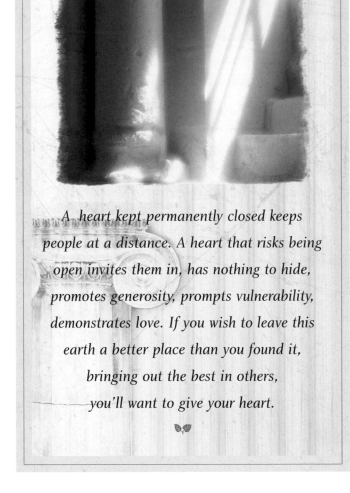

A heart kept permanently closed keeps people at a distance. A heart that risks being open invites them in, has nothing to hide, promotes generosity, prompts vulnerability, demonstrates love. If you wish to leave this earth a better place than you found it, bringing out the best in others, you'll want to give your heart.

The Ideal Gift

❧

*I*n our pocket of society, where pampered affluence is rampant, we are often at a loss to know what kind of gifts to buy our friends and loved ones on special occasions. For some people (especially those who "have everything") the standard type gift won't cut it. Nothing in the shopping mall catches our fancy.

I have a suggestion. It may not seem that expensive or sound very unique, but believe me, it works every time. It's one of those gifts that has great value but no price tag. It can't be lost nor will it ever be forgotten. No problem with size either. It fits all shapes, any age, and every personality. This ideal gift is . . . *yourself.* In your quest for character, don't forget the value of unselfishness.

THE QUEST FOR CHARACTER

Give Yourself Away

❧

Give yourself away.

Give an hour of your time to someone who needs you.

Give a note of encouragement to someone who is down.

Give a hug of affirmation to someone in your family.

Give a visit of mercy to someone who is needy.

Give a meal you prepared to someone who is sick.

Give a word of compassion to someone who is grieving.

Give a deed of kindness to someone who is overlooked.

Jesus taught: ". . . to the extent that you did it to one of these brothers of Mine, even the least of them, you did it to Me" (Matthew 25:40).

Be really generous. Give yourself away.

THE QUEST FOR CHARACTER

A Vertical Dimension

❦

Fortune says that to be successful you need to make the big bucks. Why else would the Fortune 500 list make such headlines every year? Anyone who is held up as successful must have more money than the average person.

Fame says that to be successful you need to be known in the public arena. You need to be a celebrity, a social somebody. Fame equates popularity with signicance.

Power says that to be successful you need to wield a lot of authority, flex your muscles, take charge, be in control, carry a lot of weight. Push yourself to the front.

Pleasure implies that to be successful you need to be able to do whatever feels good. This philosophy operates on the principle: "If it feels good, do it."

Fortune. Fame. Power. Pleasure. The messages bombard us from every direction. But what's missing in all this? Isn't something very significant absent here?

You bet. A *vertical* dimension. There's not even a hint of God's will or what pleases Him in the hard-core pursuit of success. Note also that nothing in that horizontal list guarantees satisfaction or brings relief deep within the heart. And in the final analysis, what most people really want in life is contentment, fulfillment, and satisfaction.

A heart filled with gratitude
cannot be anything but humble.

*Do nothing from selfishness or empty
conceit, but with humility of mind let each
of you regard one another as more important
than himself; do not merely look out for
your own personal interests, but also
for the interests of others.*

PHILIPPIANS 2:3–4

Strength of Character 🍂 122

Some Sound Advice

*If anyone thinks he is something when
he is nothing, he deceives himself.*

GALATIANS 6:3

*T*here is no greater deception than *self*-deception. It
is a tragic trap laid for everyone, but especially vulnerable
are those who have achieved success . . . and start
reading their own clippings.

Here's my advice:

1. Get a good education—but *get over it.*

2. Reach the maximum of your potential—but *don't
talk about it.*

3. Walk devotedly with God—but *don't try to look
like it.*

FIVE MEANINGFUL MINUTES A DAY

Becoming Unselfish

*H*ebrews 12:2 states, "fixing our eyes on Jesus, the author and perfecter of faith, who for the joy set before Him endured the cross, despising the shame, and has sat down at the right hand of the throne of God."

We might be tempted to think that Jesus is just the finish line and that we should only keep our eyes on Him as a runner would focus on the tape. But I think the author is urging us also to think of Jesus as the example. As the author and finisher of our faith, He not only designed the course of the race; He ran it. In fact He ran it perfectly and completely.

The Greek term *aphoraø* translated here as "fixing our eyes on" means to look exclusively at something and study it intently while consciously looking away from distractions. And the implication is imitation. Great athletes study the films of former greats to discover their techniques, to uncover any secrets to success that might offer even the slightest competitive edge. We are encouraged to go to the film vault and peer intently at one scene after another as we study Christ. "Look exclusively and thoughtfully at the One who not only designed the course but ran it flawlessly. Then run exactly as He ran." As He lived, we are to live. As He decided, we are to decide. As He obeyed, we are to obey. As He pleased the Father, we are to please the Father. As He surrendered, we are to surrender.

You want to be like Christ? Begin by thinking less about yourself. Deliberately work toward becoming unselfish. For one full day, let go of anything that serves your own interest to the exclusion of others. On that same day, fix your attention on Jesus by surrendering in complete selflessness.

So You Want to Be Like Jesus

Focusing intently on Christ naturally results in a lifestyle of increasingly greater selflessness.

Playing Second Fiddle

❦

$\mathcal{T}$he late Leonard Bernstein, composer and well-known conductor, was asked what he believed to be the most difficult instrument in the orchestra to play. He responded, "Second fiddle!"

When you examine the life of any great individual, you soon discover an entire section of second-fiddlers, super people, gifted in their own rights, but content to play their parts seated in the second chair.

FIVE MEANINGFUL MINUTES A DAY

Jesus encouraged tolerance.

*Be tolerant of those who don't look like you,
who don't dress like you, who don't care about the
things you care about, who don't vote like you.*

*Be tolerant of those whose fine points of theology
differ from yours, whose worship style is different.*

*Be tolerant of the young if you are older . . . and
be tolerant of the aging if you are young.*

*Jesus wanted His followers to be people of simple
faith, modeled in grace, based on truth.*

🍂

Wise Compromise

❦

$\mathcal{C}$ompromise is not always bad. Obviously, there are moral and ethical standards overtly taught in Scripture that leave no room whatsoever for compromise. But compromise is much broader than that. Sometimes it's wise to compromise.

Without compromise, disagreements cannot be settled. So negotiations grind to a halt. A marriage is maintained and strengthened by compromise. Moms and dads who have no wobble room are asking for trouble when the teenage years surface. Siblings who will not compromise fight. Nations with differing ideologies that refuse to listen to each other and won't compromise at various points go to war.

Am I saying it's easy? Or free from risk? Or that it comes naturally? No. It is much easier (and safer) to stand your ground . . . to keep on believing that your way is the only way to go and that your plan is the plan to follow. One major problem however . . . you wind up narrow-minded and alone, or surrounded by a few non-thinkers.

That may be safe, but it doesn't seem very satisfying. Or Christlike. While pursuing true character, don't miss wise compromise. Give your heart permission to flex!

THE QUEST FOR CHARACTER

Give Gladly!

"But when you give to the poor, do not let your
left hand know what your right hand is doing, so that
your giving will be in secret; and your Father who
sees what is done in secret will reward you."

MATTHEW 6:3–4

Give generously. Give gladly. Give sacrificially. But
keep it to yourself. Your gift is nobody's business but
yours and God's. And if you make it somebody's business,
then you immediately have your reward. You forfeit the
opportunity to receive something even greater when you
arrive in heaven. God always notices and (later) rewards
faithful, sacrificial giving. But when you insist on
announcing it in a half-dozen pious ways, then that's
all you get.

GETTING THROUGH THE TOUGH STUFF

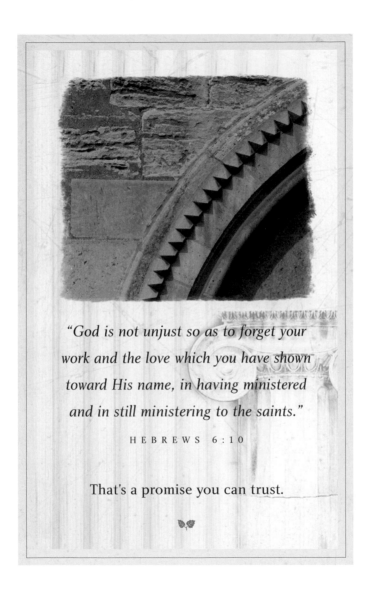

"God is not unjust so as to forget your work and the love which you have shown toward His name, in having ministered and in still ministering to the saints."

HEBREWS 6:10

That's a promise you can trust.

The Strength of
Hope

*Living hope requires
faith in the living
Lord and His Word.*

Let God be God.

Expect the unexpected.

Hope from the Heart

❧

$\mathcal{D}$o you have an unthinkable, scary, absolutely wild idea that refuses to let you sleep? That's the way it is with dreams . . . especially when God is in them. They appear crazy (they *are* crazy!). Placed alongside the triangle of logic, cost, and timing, dreams are never congruent. They won't fly when you test them against the gravity of reality. And the strangest part of all: the more they are told "can't," the more they pulsate "can" and "will" and "must."

What's behind great accomplishments? Inevitably, great people. But what is in those "great people" that makes them different? It's certainly not their age or gender or ethnicity or heritage or environment. No, it's got to be something inside their heads. They are people who *think* differently. People whose ideas are woven into a meaningful pattern on the loom of dreams, threaded with colorful strands of imagination, creativity, even a touch of fantasy.

Give your dreams room. Stay ready for anything. And I mean *anything!*

The Quest for Character

Hope Keeps Our Dreams Alive

*D*o you have a lifelong dream? Some adventurous journey you'd love to participate in . . . some discovery you long to make . . . some enterprise you secretly imagine?

Are you dreaming about writing an article or a book? Write it! Are you wondering if all that work with the kids is worth it? It's worth it. Keep pursuing. Want to go back to school and finish that degree? Go back and do it . . . pay the price, even if it takes years! Trying to master a skill that takes time, patience, and energy (not to mention money)? Press on! Thinking about going into business for yourself? Why not? It's hard to find real satisfaction halfway up someone else's corporate ladder.

Without a dream and the determination to fulfill that dream, life is quickly reduced to bleak black and wimpy white, a diet too bland to get anybody out of bed in the morning. Go after the quest that fuels your fire.

THE QUEST FOR CHARACTER

A shallow view of God leads to a shallow life.

"That's What I Call Faith!"

❦

Something down inside us admires a person who stretches our faith by doing things that are filled with vision. Initially such actions might appear to be foolish. That often occurs when we don't know the facts behind the action.

For example, I heard some time ago about a couple of nuns who worked as nurses in a hospital. They ran out of gas while driving to work one morning. A service station was nearby but had no container in which to put the needed gasoline. One of the women remembered she had a bedpan in the trunk of the car. The gas was put into the pan and they carried it very carefully back to the car. As the nuns were pouring the gasoline from the bedpan into the gas tank, two men were driving by. They stared in disbelief. Finally, one said to the other, "Now Fred, that's what I call faith!"

It appeared to be foolish. Trouble was, those doubters just didn't have the facts. And were they ever surprised when those nuns went ripping by them on the freeway!

COME BEFORE WINTER

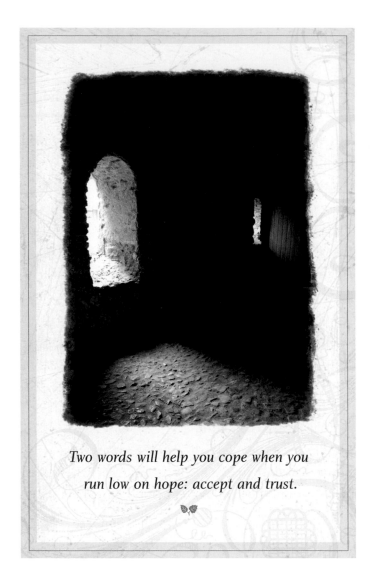

Two words will help you cope when you run low on hope: accept and trust.

A Living Hope

❧

*H*ow can we rejoice through pain? How can we have hope beyond suffering? Because we have a living hope, we have a permanent inheritance, we have divine protection, we have a developing faith, we have an unseen Savior, and we have a guaranteed deliverance.

This isn't the kind of delivery the airlines promise you when you check your bags. ("Guaranteed arrival. No problem.") I'll never forget a trip I took a few years ago. I went to Canada for a conference with plans to be there for eight days. Thanks to the airline, I only had my clothes for the last two! When I finally got my luggage, I noticed the tags on them were all marked "Berlin." ("Guaranteed arrival. No problem." They just don't guarantee when or where the bags will arrive!) That's why we now see so many people boarding airplanes with huge bags hanging from their shoulders and draped over both arms. Don't check your bags, these folks are saying, because they probably won't get there when you do.

But when it comes to spiritual delivery, we never have to worry.

HOPE AGAIN

Nothing Helps Like Hope

*H*ope is a wonderful gift from God, a source of strength and courage in the face of life's harshest trials.

- ➤ When we are trapped in a tunnel of misery, hope points to the light at the end.

- ➤ When we are overworked and exhausted, hope gives us fresh energy.

- ➤ When we are discouraged, hope lifts our spirits.

- ➤ When we are tempted to quit, hope keeps us going.

- ➤ When we lose our way and confusion blurs the destination, hope dulls the edge of panic.

- ➤ When we struggle with a crippling disease or a lingering illness, hope helps us persevere beyond the pain.

- ➤ When we fear the worst, hope brings reminders that God is still in control.

- When we must endure the consequences of bad decisions, hope fuels our recovery.

- When we find ourselves unemployed, hope tells us we still have a future.

- When we are forced to sit back and wait, hope gives us the patience to trust.

- When we feel rejected and abandoned, hope reminds us we're not alone . . . we'll make it.

- When we say our final farewell to someone we love, hope in the life beyond gets us through our grief.

Put simply, when life hurts and dreams fade, nothing helps like hope.

HOPE AGAIN

Good Plans, Great Hope

❧

Our Lord understands our limits. He realizes our struggles. He knows how much pressure we can take. He knows what measures of grace and mercy and strength we'll require. He knows how we're put together.

Frankly, His expectations are not nearly as unrealistic as ours. When we don't live up to the agenda we have set, we feel like He is going to dump a truckload of judgment on us. But that will not happen.

What, then, is God's agenda for us? Well, His plans for us are clearly set forth. He wrote them originally to Israel, but they apply to us too.

"For I know the plans that I have for you,"
declares the LORD, "plans for welfare and not
for calamity to give you a future and a hope.
Then you will call upon Me and come and
pray to Me, and I will listen to you."

JEREMIAH 29:11-12

Isn't that wonderful? "I have plans for you, My son, My daughter," God says. "And they are great plans." It is

God's agenda that His people never lose hope. Each new dawn it's as if He smiles from heaven, saying, "Hope again . . . hope again!"

HOPE AGAIN

The hope of the righteous is gladness.

PROVERBS 10:28

Worry works like bad cholesterol, hardening the arteries of our spiritual hearts and clogging the flow of love and grace toward people.

There's No Need to Worry

"Look up in the air. Look at those birds.
They don't sow. They don't reap.
They don't store food in barns."

MATTHEW 6:26

*F*rom what I've observed, those birds spend all their time in the parking lot at McDonald's. That's where the food is! And I've never seen one of them shake his head and say, "Man, I'm so worried about where that next French fry is going to come from. I mean . . . what if somebody doesn't drop his Coke this evening?" Jesus assured His listeners that our heavenly Father cares about them. He went on to point out that if He takes care of birds and flowers, certainly He will attend to our needs.

SO YOU WANT TO BE LIKE CHRIST

Everything is safe which we commit
to God, and nothing is really safe
which is not so committed.

A. W. TOZER

Have Hope!

❧

$\mathcal{G}$od has an ultimate goal in mind: that we might have hope. And what leads to such a goal? Two things: perseverance and encouragement from the Scriptures. Again, the goal is hope. God has not designed a life of despondency for us. He wants His people to have hope . . . through endurance and through encouragement from the Scriptures.

So when your hope burns low, when people disappoint you, when events turn against you, when dreams die, when the walls close in, when the prognosis seems grim, when your heart breaks, *look at the Lord, and keep on looking at Him.*

We never know when our disappointment will be His appointment.

God likes surprises. Breaking molds is His specialty.

Five Meaningful Minutes a Day

All of us need encouragement—
somebody to believe in us. To reassure
and reinforce us. To help us pick up
the pieces and go on. To help us
hope in spite of the odds.

Vote "Yes"!

❦

*A*lmost every day—certainly every week—we encounter someone who is in his or her own boat, thinking seriously about sailing on the most daring, most frightening voyage of a lifetime. That soul may be a friend, your marriage partner, someone you work with, a neighbor, perhaps a family member. The ocean of possibilities is enormously inviting yet, let's face it, terribly threatening. Urge them on! Vote "Yes"! Shout a rousing "You are really something . . . I'm proud of you!" Dare to say what they need to hear the most, "Go for it!" Then pray like mad.

Sometimes our problem is not a lack of potential, it's a lack of perseverance . . . not a problem of having the goods but of hearing the bads. How very much could be accomplished if only there were more brave souls on the end of the pier urging us on, affirming us, encouraging us to hope, regardless of the risks.

THE QUEST FOR CHARACTER

The Strength of
Sincerity

*God is not impressed
with externals. He always
focuses on the inward qualities.*

God is holy. Exalted. He is the only wise
God, the Creator, the Maker, the sovereign
Lord. He is the Master. He tells me what to do,
and I have no safe option but to do it. There
is no alternative, no multiple choices. We have
but one directive, and that is to do His will.

Genuine Sincerity

That you may approve the things that are excellent, in
order to be sincere and blameless until the day of Christ.

PHILIPPIANS 1:10

We who desire to develop character must allow
sincerity to be our badge of excellence. *Sincere* is actually
a Latin word, meaning "without wax." The Greek term
means "sun-tested." The ancients had a very fine porcelain
that was greatly valued and therefore expensive. Often,
when fired in the kiln tiny cracks would appear. Dishonest
merchants would smear pearly-white wax over these
cracks, which would pass for unblemished porcelain—
unless held up to the light of the sun. Honest dealers
marked their flawless wares *sine cera*—"without wax."

That is genuine sincerity. No sham, no hypocrisy.
No hidden cracks to be covered over. The absence of
cracks guarantees the presence of truth. When true
sincerity flows from our lives we are then "like Christ."

THE QUEST FOR CHARACTER

Alive to God's Power

I love the story of the missionary who sailed from Liverpool, England, to serve Christ along the African coast. He changed vessels at Lagos, Nigeria. There he boarded a coastal tugboat to make his way into a fever-infested region where he would invest the rest of his life. While changing vessels, he came upon a cynical old slave trader who looked critically on the man's decision by saying, "If you go to that place, you will die." The missionary, a devoted Christian, replied softly, "I died before I ever left Liverpool."

Not until you and I know that we are dead to sin's control and alive to God's power through Christ will we live like victors, not victims.

THE GRACE AWAKENING

*Jesus came and ministered in a new and
different way—full of grace and full of
truth, He introduced a revolutionary,
different way of life.*

Living in the Light

❧

When we actively engage in sin, we consciously put aside what we know to be the truth about God. We lie to ourselves by saying, "We'll get by. God won't mind so much."

You can live as you please if you know you're not being seen and you won't get caught. But if, down deep inside, you *know* there is a living and holy God who will not let you get away with sin, you will avoid sin at all cost. That is exactly what the Lord wanted to establish first with the people of Israel—a holy, righteous, pure, and respectful concept of His presence.

When you come to that understanding, and God's light breaks into your life like the pure whitewater of a rushing river, you learn to thoroughly hate and dread those actions that will plunge you again into darkness.

Moses: A Man of Selfless Dedication

Single-Minded Sincerity

He who doubts is . . . a double-minded
man, unstable in all his ways.

JAMES 1:6, 8 NKJV

*D*ouble-mindedness is a common disease that leaves its victims paralyzed by doubt . . . hesitant, hypocritical, full of theoretical words, but lacking in confident action. Lots of talk but no guts. Insincere and insecure.

How much better to be single-minded! No mumbo-jumbo. No religious phony-baloney. No say-one-thing-but-mean-something-else jive.

The single-minded are short on creeds and long on deeds.

They care . . . *really* care.

They are humble . . . *truly* humble.

They love . . . *genuinely* love.

They have character . . . *authentic* character.

THE QUEST FOR CHARACTER

Lord of reality
make me real—
not plastic,
synthetic,
pretend phony;
an actor playing out his part,
hypocrite.

JOSEPH BAYLY

True Faith

❧

Stories from the underground church in Russia never fail to jolt us awake. Many years ago a house church in a city of the former Soviet Union received one copy of the Gospel by Luke, the only Scripture most of these Christians had ever seen. They tore it into small sections and distributed them among the body of believers. Their plan was to memorize the portion they had been given, then on the next Lord's Day they would meet and redistribute the scriptural sections.

On Sunday these believers arrived inconspicuously in small groups throughout the day so as not to arouse the suspicion of KGB informers. By dusk they were all safely inside, windows closed and doors locked. They began by singing a hymn quietly but with deep emotion. Suddenly, the door was pushed open and in walked two soldiers with loaded automatic weapons at the ready. One shouted, "All right—everybody line up against the wall. If you wish to renounce your commitment to Jesus Christ, leave now!"

Two or three quickly left, then another. After a few more seconds, two more.

"This is your last chance. Either turn against your faith in Christ," he ordered, "or stay and suffer the consequences."

Another left. Finally, two more in embarrassed silence with their faces covered slipped out into the night. No one else moved. Parents with small children trembling beside them looked at them reassuringly. They fully expected to be gunned down or, at best, to be imprisoned.

After a few moments of complete silence, the other soldier closed the door, looked back at those who stood against the wall and said, "Keep your hands up—but this time in praise to our Lord Jesus Christ, brothers and sisters. We, too, are Christians. We were sent to another house church several weeks ago to arrest a group of believers—"

The other soldier interrupted, ". . . but, instead, *we were converted!* We have learned by experience, however, that unless people are willing to die for their faith, they cannot be fully trusted."

LIVING ABOVE THE LEVEL OF MEDIOCRITY

God has no limitations in His ability
to pull something off, but He's going
to do it in His time and not before.

In the Shadow of the Cross

❧

$\mathcal{G}$od's success is never contrived. It is never forced. It is never the working of human flesh. It is usually unexpected—and its benefits are always surprising.

The hand of God holds you firmly in His control. The hand of God casts a shadow of the cross across your life. Sit down at the foot of that cross and deliberately submit your soul to His mighty hand. Accept His discipline. Acknowledge His deliverance. Ask for His discernment.

Then be quiet. Be still. Wait. And move over so I can sit beside you. I'm waiting too.

HOPE AGAIN

God's Will, God's Way

It is one thing to do the will of God. It is another thing entirely to do it God's way in God's time.

Let's make it a little more personal. God has made it clear to you that He neither desires nor requires you to remain single. He knows you are lonely, knows you do not possess the gift of celibacy, and knows that time is passing and prospects are narrowing.

At some point, if you do not guard your heart, you may say to the Lord, in effect, "Okay, God, I know Your plan. You want me married. Now, please just step aside for a few months. When I get to the altar, I'll whistle. At that time, I'd like You to come back and bless the union, and we'll slip back into Your plans and pursue Your will."

You see how that works? You say you want the will of God, but through manipulation, compromise, matchmaking, and game-playing, you get the one of your choice. Only then do you suddenly rediscover God and pray, "O Lord, please bless this union. Make it strong and great because, as You have led me, I am getting married today."

Although you want to do the will of God, if you are bent on carrying out that plan in your own way, taking matters into your own hands, you will wind up losing His blessing. Remember this motto:

I try, I fail.

I trust, He succeeds!

Only eight words, yet how profound. Bottom line: If you are moving in the energy of the flesh, you're doomed to fail.

MOSES: A MAN OF SELFLESS DEDICATION

Sincerely Submitted to God

❧

*Humble yourselves, therefore, under the mighty hand
of God, that He may exalt you at the proper time.*

1 PETER 5:6

W hat does it mean to humble *yourself* under the mighty
hand of God in *your* job, vocation, or profession? What if
you're not getting the raise or the promotion you deserve?
What if you are in a situation where you could make things
happen . . . but you really want God to do that?

Think of David, the young musician, tending his
father's sheep back on the hills of Judea many centuries
ago. He was a self-taught, gifted musician. He didn't hire
an agent and go on tour, trying to make a name for himself. Instead, he sang to the sheep. He had no idea that
someday his lyrics would find their way into the psalter
or would be the very songs that have inspired and com-
forted millions of people through long and dark nights.

David didn't seek success; he simply humbled himself
under the mighty hand of God, staying close to the Lord
and submitting himself to Him. And in His time God
exalted David to the highest position in the land. He
became the shepherd of the entire nation!

HOPE AGAIN

Living Transformed

🦋

*I*n today's terms, that proud Pharisee known as Saul of Tarsus won all the marbles—the Pulitzer, the Medal of Honor, the Most Valuable Player, the Heisman, the Gold Medal . . . the Nobel of Ancient Jewry. Had they had newspapers or magazines in his day, his picture would have been on the front page, and the headlines would have read, RELIGIOUS ZEALOT OF THE DECADE. His was the name dropped by everybody who was anybody. Any search for a model to follow would have led to the scholar from Tarsus, but you would have to move fast to keep up. He wasn't nearly finished with his plan to rid the world of Christians. The last entry in his Daytimer read, "Next stop: Damascus." On that fateful trip, everything changed.

While riding the crest of that wave of international fame, Saul of Tarsus met his match in the person of Jesus Christ. While still on the outskirts of the city of Damascus, he was suddenly struck blind by a blazing light from heaven and silenced by a voice that must have sounded like the roar of a dozen Niagaras: "Saul . . . Saul . . . why are you persecuting Me?" Though blinded by the light, at that moment the Pharisee got his first glimpse of perfect righteousness. And for the first time in his life he was humbled. His robes of self-righteousness were nothing more than filthy rags. All his trophies and plaques and impressive earthly honors were as worthless as wood, hay, and stubble. One glimpse of true, heaven-sent righteousness was enough to convince him forever that he had spent his entire life on the wrong road traveling at breakneck speed in the wrong direction for all the wrong reasons.

His entire frame of reference was altered. His whole perspective changed. His way of thinking and, of course, his way of life were radically transformed from that day forward. His dreams of making it all on his own were forever dashed on the solid rock of Jesus Christ. That was the day Paul really started to live.

LAUGH AGAIN

Mark it down, things do not "just happen."
Ours is not a random, whistle-in-the-dark
universe. There is a God-arranged plan for
this world of ours, which includes a specific
plan for you. And through every ordinary
day and every extraordinary moment, there
is a God who constantly seeks you.

Paul's sincere desire in life was:

*"That I may know Him—that I may
progressively become more deeply and
intimately acquainted with Him, perceiving and
recognizing and understanding [the wonders
of His person] more strongly and clearly."*

PHILIPPIANS 3:1
AMPLIFIED NEW TESTAMENT

What is your sincere desire?

_____

_____

_____

_____

_____

God-Centered

$\mathcal{A}$sk people around the coffee pot at work what "godliness" means and see what kind of answers you get. Some picture a monk removed from the challenges of the world, studying, praying, meditating, humming outdated chants behind the walls of a monastery. Others see a squeaky-clean, Bible-toting, do-gooder. Naïve, moralistic . . . annoyingly innocent. . . .

More accurately, a "godly" person is one who ceases to be self-centered in order to become God-centered. Christ became a man and, as a result of His earthly ministry, we see how God intended for humans to behave. Jesus is our unblemished example of godliness. Therefore, a godly person is a Christlike person.

So You Want to Be Like Christ

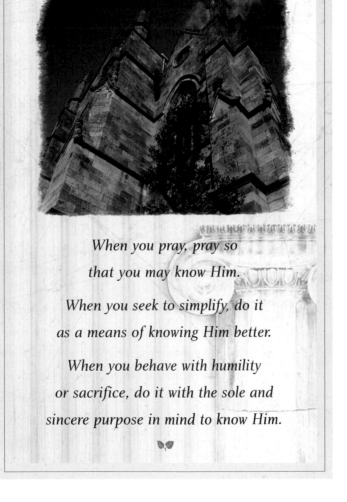

When you pray, pray so
that you may know Him.

When you seek to simplify, do it
as a means of knowing Him better.

When you behave with humility
or sacrifice, do it with the sole and
sincere purpose in mind to know Him.

Asking and Learning

*L*et me give you a little help on getting through the tough stuff of personal misunderstanding. Three simple thoughts come to mind. Because they have worked for me, I offer them to you.

1. *When misunderstood, ask "who?"* This is the age-old advice of considering the source. Jesus responded to misunderstanding by seeing Himself through other people's eyes. Each time that helped Him grasp why they saw Him as they did and how He should respond. Asking "who?" is a good place to start.

2. *If misunderstanding continues, ask "why?"* You may be misunderstood because of something you're doing inadvertently. We all have blind spots that keep us from seeing the whole picture . . . the way others see us. If you are often misunderstood on the same point, you'd be wise to examine why. We all need to examine ourselves from time to time. Asking why is healthy.

3. *When misunderstanding is resolved, ask "what?"*
   What can you learn from the experience? Could
   you have responded to the situation in a more
   mature manner? Have you owned your mistakes?
   Are you sure there are no other bases to cover?
   Learning from misunderstanding can help prevent
   future pain and anguish.

GETTING THROUGH THE TOUGH STUFF

*Do you realize how closely unity and
humility are tied together? Like Siamese
twins, neither can exist without the other.*

How refreshing to step back in the
shadows of our insignificance and give
full attention to the greatness of God.

Sincere Spirituality

❧

$\mathcal{T}$hough we've promised ourselves and the Lord it would be different this year, many of us continue to wrestle with a stubborn, eight-armed octopus called "busy-ness." We continually find ourselves pushing too hard, going too fast, trying to do too much. Am I right? The "tyranny of the urgent" has wrapped its powerful tentacles around yet another year, hasn't it? Even though you know that the secret of knowing God requires "being still" (Psalm 46:10—the original Hebrew language says, *Cease striving—let go, relax!*), you've already started rationalizing your busy-ness. But by doing so, you have put the development of character on hold.

Do you realize the dangers of a life without privacy? Are you aware that a lack of time to be alone with God initiates spiritual disintegration?

To be used of God. Is there anything more encouraging, more fulfilling? Perhaps not, but there is something more basic: to meet with God, to linger in His presence, to shut out the noise of the world.

THE QUEST FOR CHARACTER

Closing
Thoughts

God's got our future, our circumstances,
our friends, and our foes in His
hands and under His control.

A Heart of Wisdom

Teach us to number our days aright,

that we may gain a heart of wisdom.

PSALM 90:12 NIV

$\mathcal{T}$he original Hebrew text suggests that we correctly "account" for our days. I find it interesting that we are to view life by the days, not *the years*. We are to live those days in such a way that when they draw to a close, we have gained "a heart of wisdom." With the Lord God occupying first place in our lives we accept and live each day enthusiastically for Him. The result will be that "heart of wisdom."

STRENGTHENING YOUR GRIP

Willing to Do God's Will

*"I glorified You on the earth, having
accomplished the work which
You have given Me to do."*

J O H N   1 7 : 4

I have often thought of Jesus' words when He was
only hours removed from the cross. In His prayer to the
Father, . . . He said, "I glorified You on the earth, having
accomplished the work which You have given Me to do"
(John 17:4). A little over thirty-three years after His
arrival in Bethlehem, there He stood in Jerusalem,
saying, in effect, "It's a wrap." He had done everything
the Father sent Him to do . . . and in the final analysis,
that's what mattered.

FIVE MEANINGFUL MINUTES A DAY

The closer we walk with the Lord, the less

control we have over our own lives, and

the more we must abandon to Him.

*Not one fleeting moment of life goes by
without God's knowing exactly where we are,
what we're doing, and how we're feeling.*

God Is at Work in You!

❦

*T*hroughout our days—year after year—the lifelong process of character development goes on. While we wait, God works. So let's not grow weary. The more He hammers and files, shapes and chisels, the more we are being conformed to the image of His Son. Be patient. Trust Him even in the pain, even though the process is long.

When life seems like a jungle of difficulties and disappointments, when times are hard and people are demanding, never forget that life is *special*. All of life. The pleasurable days as well as the painful ones. The Wednesdays as well as the weekends. The holidays as well as the days after. Days that seem insignificant and boring just as much as those when we get to see the President or receive a promotion or win a marathon. Every single day is a special day.

God is at work in you. And with God at work, you are in for the time of your life!

Acknowledgments

❦

$\mathcal{G}$ rateful acknowledgment is made to the following
publishers for permission to reprint this copyrighted
material. All copyrights are held by the author,
Charles R. Swindoll.

Living Above the Level of Mediocrity (Nashville:
W Publishing Group, 1981).

The Quest for Character (Sisters, Oregon: Multnomah,
1987)

Come Before Winter and Share my Hope (Grand Rapids:
Zondervan, 1988)

The Grace Awakening (Nashville: W Publishing Group,
1990)

Laugh Again (Nashville: W Publishing Group, 1994)

Hope Again (Nashville: W Publishing Group, 1996)

David: A Man of Passion and Destiny (Nashville: W Publishing Group, 1997)

The Mystery of God's Will (Nashville: W Publishing Group, 1999)

Moses: A Man of Selfless Dedication (Nashville: W Publishing Group, 1999)

Five Meaningful Minutes a Day (Nashville: J Countryman, 2003)

Strengthening Your Grip (Nashville: W Publishing, 2003)

Job: A Man of Heroic Endurance (Nashville: W Publishing, 2004)

Getting Through the Tough Stuff (Nashville: W Publishing, 2004)

So, You Want to Be Like Christ? (Nashville: W Publishing, 2005)